ROGET'S ILLUSION

ALSO BY LINDA BIERDS

Flight: New and Selected Poems (2008)

First Hand (2005)

The Seconds (2001)

The Profile Makers (1997)

The Ghost Trio (1994)

Heart and Perimeter (1991)

The Stillness, the Dancing (1988)

Flights of the Harvest-Mare (1985)

Linda Bierds

....

ROGET'S ILLUSION

....

A MARIAN WOOD BOOK

Published by G. P. Putnam's Sons

a member of Penguin Group (USA)

New York

PUTNAM

A MARIAN WOOD BOOK
Published by G. P. Putnam's Sons
Publishers Since 1838
Published by the Penguin Group
Penguin Group (USA) LLC
375 Hudson Street
New York, New York 10014

USA • Canada • UK • Ireland • Australia
New Zealand • India • South Africa • China

penguin.com
A Penguin Random House Company

Library of Congress Cataloging-in-Publication Data

Bierds, Linda.
[Poems. Selections]
Roget's Illusion / Linda Bierds.
p.   cm.
Includes bibliographical references.
"A Marian Wood Book."
ISBN 978-0-399-16546-7
I. Title.
PS3552.I357A6   2014
811'.54—dc23   201303715

Printed in the United States of America
1   3   5   7   9   10   8   6   4   2

BOOK DESIGN BY AMANDA DEWEY

This book is printed on acid-free paper. ∞

Once again, for Sydney

Acknowledgments

Grateful acknowledgment is made to the following magazines where these poems first appeared, some in a slightly earlier form:

American Poet: The Journal of the Academy of American Poets, "Navigation"; *The Atlantic Monthly*, "On Reflection," "Simulacra," "Sketchbook"; *Bellingham Review*, "Exhibition of a Rhinoceros at Venice"; *Blackbird*, "Meriwether and the Magpie"; *Borderlands: Texas Poetry Review*, "Girl in a Dove-Gray Dress," "Pavo"; *Field*, "Salvage"; *Fifth Wednesday Journal*, "Darwin's Mirror"; *Gulf Coast*, "Notes from Prehistory"; *The Journal*, "Pierrots, Slightly Leaning: Brighton, 1915, Venice, 1903," "Steller's Jay," "Thoughts Toward the First Christmas Lecture"; *The Laurel Review*, "Dürer near Fifty"; *New England Review*, "The Swifts"; *Northwest Review*, "From the Sea of Tranquillity"; *Poem-A-Day* (Academy of American Poets), "Incomplete Lioness"; *Poetry*, "Accountancy: Dürer in Antwerp," "Flight"; *Poetry Northwest*, "Correlation of the Physical Forces,"

"Fragments from Venice: Albrecht Dürer," "From Campalto"; *The Seattle Review*, "Enthusiasm"; *TSR: The Southampton Review*, "The Moths"; *Water~Stone Review*, "The Shepherd's Horn."

"Accountancy: Dürer in Antwerp" and "The Swifts" were reprinted in *Poetry Daily*; "1918 Huber Light Four" was issued in a limited-edition broadside published by Brooding Heron Press, Waldron Island, Washington.

Thanks also to *The Alhambra Poetry Calendar* for reprinting a number of these poems: "Accountancy: Dürer in Antwerp" (2008), "Navigation" (2009), "Notes from Prehistory" (2010), "The Moths" (2011), "Pavo" (2012), "Darwin's Mirror" (2013).

CONTENTS

Part One

Part Two

Part Three

•   •   •   *This symbol is used to indicate a space between stanzas when such space
is lost in pagination.*

PART ONE

Roget's Illusion: One

· PETER MARK ROGET, 1779–1869

Best known for gradations of language

and not for the carriage wheel spinning beyond

a picket fence, *its curious optical deception.*

Best known for the word-on-word columns I follow,

semblance to *severance,* *biography* to *bracken,*

his synonyms, antonyms, metonyms, idioms,

and not for his paper on

wheel spokes glimpsed through vertical apertures.

Remarkable, he wrote. *Puzzling. Wondrous*—

how carriage spokes rolling past fence slats

seem to be still or turning backward, or, better still,

completely gone. On his desk, near medical texts

and a swan-neck lamp, a quarter-scale

wooden human figure catches sunlight

down its polished spine, the model

best used for anatomy lessons

and not as a paperweight

keeping his entries on *Time* and *Causation*

away from his entries on carriage wheels.

Although paperweight is its purpose now,

a sunlit, seated, boxwood shape

slumped on the soft thesaurus, which, like

history or yeast, swells with each passing hour.

The whole is unachievable, he wrote.

Uncontainable, the catalogue and turning wheel.

Best seen through slats and apertures, columns

and vacancies. The rotating illusion.

Best visited in slanted light, when the parts

are oblique on their shadows,

and spokes and broken syllables

send luminous, curved lines

that convey the impression of unbrokenness . . .

Simulacra

Before the beak of a tiny pipette
dipped through a glisten of DNA
and ewe quickened to ewe
with exactly the simulacrum
forty thousand years had worked toward,
before Muybridge's horses cantered
and a ratchet-and-pawl-cast waltzing couple
shuffled along a phasmatrope,
before dime-size engines
sparked in the torsos of toddler dolls
and little bellows let them sing
and the Unassisted Walking One—
Miss Autoperipatetikos—stepped
in her caterpillar gait
across the New World's wide-plank floor,
before motion moved the figures, and torsion
moved the motion—or steam, or sand,
or candle flame—before magnets and taut springs
nudged Gustav the Climbing Miller
up his mill's retaining wall (and gravity

retrieved him), before image, like sound,

stroked through an outreach of crests and troughs,

and corresponding apertures

caught patterns in the waves,

caught, like eels beneath ancestral ponds,

radiance in the energy,

before lamposcope and zograscope,

fantascope and panorama, before lanterns

re-cast human hands, or a dye-drop

of beetle first fluttered across

a flicker book of papyrus leaves,

someone sketched a creature along the contours

of a cave, its stippled, monochromatic shape

tracing the vaults and hollows,

shivers of flank and shoulder

already drawing absence nearer,

as torchlight set the motion

and shadow set the rest.

Notes from Prehistory

• FONT-DE-GAUME CAVE PAINTINGS, LES EYZIES, FRANCE

At Font-de-Gaume, the bison—eighty—

bulge outward from their spindle legs

and, quickened by candlelight, inch a half-step closer

to flint-carved human hands and nineteen

tectiforms. Across the cave, sketched

to trace its contour lines, two dozen mammoths stir.

And oxen—eight. Four capridae. One feline. (Two?)

One bear. Not white, of course, although

calcitic film, spawned across the centuries,

has powdered it. Not violet-mouthed. Not

iceberg-drawn, walking past the confluence

of James and Hudson Bays, out and out, the ice

too sparse, a thin, chivalric cape

laid down on the endless water.

Six varied signs. Or five. Cone. Canopy.

Headless ampersand, swirled by lichen and manganese.

Not nebular, those swirls, not polychrome,

not cast in sheets across a bay, solar-flared,

electric, green on muted red.
One slender tri-forked cave, thin-branched as a sapling.
One Rubicon. One terminal diverticulum.

One bear, quickened in place, stopped
on a lozenge of stone, a shrinking,
fissure-crafted raft, above a canopy,
beneath an ampersand. Here—and there—
the stone, like ice, is water-polished
or scoured by flint to a silver sheen, scratch marks
zigging this way and that.

Like magic, a candle's light would shape
the marks—erratic, pin-thin lines drawn up
to concentric rings. Illusion, of course. Mirage.
Not symmetry. Not grace.
Just flint and form and a resin torch:
to venerate the living world
and keep the ghosts at bay.

Dürer near Fifty

At dawn on Saint Barbara's Eve, just below
the plateau of his fiftieth year, Albrecht Dürer, first
having purchased spectacles, shoes, and an ivory button,
rode a wheel-etched swath of longitude
from Antwerp toward Zeeland, where a whale—
one hundred fathoms long—pulsed on the dark sand.
First having purchased snuffers and furnace-brown,
and coated the pages of his silverpoint sketchbook,
where his scratch lines—like pears, or tarnish, or thought—
would gradually ripen, he circled Zeeland's seven shores,
past Goes and Wolfersdyk and *the sunken place*
where rooftops stood up from the water.
Already, from thought, he had sketched a dozen
tail-locked sirens, and once, gossip's composite,
a paisleyed rhinoceros with a dorsal horn—and so
would see firsthand a whale, having changed in Antwerp
a Philips florin, and dined with the Portuguese,
and studied the bones of the giant, Antigoon—
his shoulder blade wider than a strong man's back—
although, in fact, the bones were whale, while the whale

Dürer sailed toward was history, erased by degrees

on the outgoing tide. Still, history tells us,

from his spot on that salty prow, Dürer drew precisely

the unseen sight: the absent arc of its sunken shape,

the absent fluke and down-turned eye,

even, it appears, the absent trench the acid sea

had bitten so seamlessly back into the world.

Sketchbook

· DR. NICOLAAS TULP, 1635

Because, each week, he has entered the body,

its torso, freshly sanitized, its legs and arteries,

the rose curve on the underchin executed so deftly

by the hangman's rope; because he has entered

the forearm and cortex, the lobes and hidden

vortices, deeper, then deeper, until what remains—

shallow, undissected flesh—seems simple lines,

their one dimension shadowless;

and because he is tired and has been himself

a subject,

       Tulp crumples his page, then tries again

to sketch a caged orangutan. Placid, insouciant,

the animal slips its shallow glances upward,

downward, from the white-ruffed shape shaping it

to the lap and simple page, as the first lines quicken

and a ratted brow begins. There, a nostril,

and there, a shadowing, a depth that plumps

the cheek pouch, the finger's wrinkled

vortices. Slumped at their separate walls, neither
meets the other's eyes,

                    although, equally, each
completes the circling gaze—man to beast to page
to man: two pelt-and-pipesmoke-scented curves,
dimensionless, mammalian. Tick by tick
the minutes pass, page by crumpled page.
Beyond the door, caws and yelps and the clack
of carriage wheels . . . and still they sit,
Tulp, the ape, content to see the shapes
they've known—or felt, or sensed, or turned within—
sloughed in husks across the straw.

Fragments from Venice:
Albrecht Dürer

You write for news and Venetian vellum.

I answer: From the sea today a mystery:
proportion's carapaced nightmare: lobster.

You write for burnt glass.

I answer: When tides cross San Marco's cobbles,
bare-shouldered women, bare-shouldered girls,
walk planks to the dark cathedral.

Herr Willibald, my French mantle greets you!
My plumes and misgivings greet you!
Blue-black near the boiling vat, my carapaced neighbor
greets you! (Since dusk, his thin-stalked eyes, like sunflowers,
have tracked my orbiting candle.)

. . .

You write that my altarpiece
cups in its wings our destinies.

I answer: In one-point perspective, all lines converge
in a dot of sun far out on the earth's horizon.

I answer: Nightfall makes centaurs of the gondoliers.

I answer: Afloat through the inns, a second perspective
transposes the reign of earth and sun, placing *us*
at the vanishing point.

You write that stubble on the winter fields
supports, through frost, a second field.

I answer: When tides withdraw there are birthmarks
on the cobbles. And on the girls' satin slippers
age-rings of silt.

You have seen, secondhand, the centaurs.

I have seen the lobster redden,
then rise like a sun through the boiling water.

. . .

Immortality's sign? you ask me. That slow-gaited sea change?
That languorous rising?

I have also seen a comet cross the sky.

From the Sea of Tranquillity

Item: After the hopping and gathering,
in that flat, crepuscular light, Armstrong
stroked to the moon's crisp dust, it is said,
Albrecht Dürer's initials, first the A's wide table,
then beneath it, the slumped, dependable D,
the image sinking slowly through that waterless sea,
named less for tides than resemblances.

Item: In the year 1471, in the sixth hour
of Saint Prudentia's Day, Albrecht Dürer was born,
the moon afloat in Gemini's house, and far to the east
Leo rising; an alliance that promised, with travel
and wealth, a slender physique—so slender, in fact,
Dürer slipped from it daily, as, gripped by concentration,
someone else's Albrecht drew a stylus down the grain.

Item: Kicked up through the moon's pale dust, a boot
creates not a scattering but a wave, particles joined
in a singular motion, faithful to the shape

of displacement. Such is the loss of atmosphere,

although aura remains, and time. Think of two men,

each at his milky page, thirst and the dipper

a moment away, and the whole unbroken before them.

Pavo

• PAVO, N. (L. *PEACOCK*) A CONSTELLATION OF THE SOUTHERN SKY

Long before the fast and truss, they named the horse

for the mine, Pavo, drawn to the word's pulse,

its hoof-tap and sigh, as miners all down

the rocky divide were drawn to the tappings and sighs,

the mines and their names, the history they climbed

like strata: Vulcan, Argonaut, Mayflower, Buffalo,

Blue-Jay, Orphan Boy, Moonlight.

                           Pavo, they said—

for peacock, for copper, the peacock of ores—

Easy, as they knotted the blindfold and draped him

in grommeted leather, then rigged him fore-and-aft,

back hooves toward chest, front hooves toward belly,

then hoisted him upright to the lift's slim cage

and slipped him tail first through the earth,

two, three, four thousand feet.

                           One century

before today, our cinched space and water-filled moon,

when the adit was cut and far down the drifts

stringers of air replaced stringers of ore,

and mystery began, as it always does—tommy-knockers

and candle auguries—they untrussed the truss,

refolded the blindfold, watched as he kicked three times

then stilled,

      as filled with unknowing as they once were,

fresh from the lift.

         Long before

a flagpole's weightless nib pierced the lunar dust

and pumice shattered, and rovers flexed

their divining rods, the miners approached

the gaunted horse, their hair green-tinted

from copper seep,

         their jumper coats scummed

from some synthesis of world and rain.

Bedrock. Primer. Seedling. Canopy . . . Where to begin,

they wondered, then began as they always do,

as they touched, then lowered, the long head,

first to the water, then to the grain.

Flight

Osseous, aqueous, cardiac, hepatic—
back from bone the echoes stroke, back
from the halved heart, the lungs
three years of weightlessness have cinched to gills.
From a leather chaise, the astronaut's withered legs
dangle, as back they come, sounds
a beaked percussion hammer startles into shape.
The physician cocks his head and taps—exactly
as a splitter halves his slate, the metamorphic rock
chisel-shocked, then shocked again, halved

and halved, until a roof appears, black as space.
I'm gaining ground, he says, the astronaut,
who knows, from space, earth is just a blue-green glow,
a pilot light he circled once, lifted, swiftly flown
above the rafters and atmospheres, half himself
and half again some metamorphic click,
extinct as memory. I'm gaining ground,

he says, and back it comes, his glint

of cloud-crossed world: a pilot light

or swaddled leaf, green in the season's infancy.

1918 Huber Light Four

To say that it glowed,

the tractor's half-scale replica,

its twenty polished woods seamless and separate

as a tract of furrows filled with rain,

is to offer the finish before the start,

the worm before the jig. Yet to say late sun,

cast through the fair's barn-turned-exhibition-hall,

burnished it, as it burnished

the jars of yellow beets, shifts agency

to a higher power. Three years, the woodworker said,

two thousand hours drawing walnut's brindled light,

and whatever light the willow offered,

the cedar and birch, the African mahogany.

Almost alchemy, how sanding transformed

wood to grain. Almost chemistry: friction, air,

vapors beneath the polish cloth—almost

. . .

complete combustion, the perfect half-scale whole of it
clean as the flames some candles offer. Though to say
that it drew from its absent shape,
as candles do, suggests a labor less touched

by time, or a time less touched by absence.
Hour by hour, something like harmony
passed through the room, while something like melanin
rose in the model's polished wood,

in the Kalif dahlias and sawdust floor, then darkened
a tabletop tapestry, the spokes of grain and braided vines
arranged like a living wagon wheel,
and darkened the wheel hub's gathered quince

and a slender ripple of cornsilk wind—
illusion's ancient artifact:
thin strands stretching out from a back-cast rim
to show that a stillness was turning.

PART TWO

Roget's Illusion: Two

Before *Confinement* and *Preservation*,
in the columns beside *cart wheel* and *gear*,
he has written *compass . . . windlass . . . hinge*—
all above *Evolution* but below *Elevation*.

And in columns beyond *cart wheel* and *gear*,
a thousand synonyms bleat, as his weary mind,
above revolution but below revelation,
wishes the project penned. Even cribbed. Bound

for a thousand weary minds. The metonyms bleat
for the animal world, just outside his window,
cribbed, penned, bound, projected into wisdoms
the stars align across. He stops, watches two moths,

just outside the window, whirl toward his lamp's minimal
light. Why try again to capture *Matter* or *Symmetry*,
when the line he watches from stars to lamp stops
in a moth-shaped cipher of dust?

. . .

Lamp. Matter. Symmetry. Why try again to capture
the world? Light as compass, wind as hinge?
All the dust-shaped moths on their word-shaped pins,
after *Confinement* and before *Preservation*?

The Evening Star

Full night not yet on the Sound
and far to the west, one brilliant, snow-filled mountain
flares over the water toward me, its quick afterimage
fluttering behind, part peak, part half-transparent moth
skimming the table
                    and reference books,
stitching together the weathered lines
where Dürer sketches Adam's ash tree, and Kepler
watches a dead star's light, and someone
named Smeaton——John——hauls a tallow-fed chandelier
up the lighthouse steps near Plymouth.

Plump, short-winged, retinal burn, pulsing
over the flat-lined past, reviving
the burins and waxy Edens, the breezes and tides,
the twenty-four half-pound chandelier candles
slowly slipping their lighthouse beam
down another century's hazards.
                    And then it's gone,

quick sprinkle of ash dusting a membrane's rods and cones.

Everything still, again. The sun just down, the past

just words, and the first starlight so pale

on the dusk, I must turn to catch it peripherally.

Thoughts Toward
the First Christmas Lecture

· MICHAEL FARADAY, 1860

A skin of ice on the inner panes
and Faraday there at the window, his candle flame
burning a peephole. Already morning has warmed
the eaves, the hedgerows thickened by snow.
Children, he thinks, penless, his words underscored
by a tendril of smoke, *I speak to you as a child myself,*
amazed by the candle's phenomena: wax and light
and uplifting air, the little cup they form together,
the shallow pool that shivers there. Over
an empty hummock, parallel tracks of a sleigh soften,
and between the tracks, a horse's widening hoofprints.
Something has scurried across that journey—marten
or hare—bisecting the sleigh tracks. *Consider*
that grand circularity, light to fuel to light.
And mystery: a flame that never bites the host
but fattens from it nonetheless. Perhaps there were
two horses, stepping in tandem down the hummock,
one set of hoofprints absorbing the other. *Children,*

we are drawn here to be philosophers, to ask always,

What is the cause? And so you question,

How do flame and fuel meet? And so I say,

By mutual attraction. By the bonding of things

undissolved in each other. Unlikely, of course, still

were their gaits equal and the reins crossed

their shoulders simultaneously. . . . *Let us turn*

to an illustration. Tip your towel to a basin of water,

or better—better!—trouble your mother for a fresh prawn,

then place it tail first in a tumbler, plump head

cupped over the rim. Children, water will climb

through the creature—as fuel climbs a wick!—

by mutual attraction. Already morning

has warmed the eaves, the icicles transparent now,

sloughing their waxy frost—and soon to be prisms,

blinding, as the sun arcs into view. *And what of the flame,*

you ask me, its shadow so solid on the classroom wall?

How can it be both substance and light? Perhaps

there were two horses, stepping in tandem

down the white expanse—soon to be blinding . . .

Children, I must leave you for now with this:

Never is flame of a single body, but a multitude of

successions, so rapid the eye unites them as one.

Something has scurried across the sleigh tracks—

marten or hare—its jittery flight bisecting the hummock,

this way—or that—its slim path both absence and shape,

a low-slung whip of smoke.

Navigation

Waves or Moths or whatever it is to be called.

· VIRGINIA WOOLF

If it is to be The Waves, then
the moon, perhaps, weighting a sextant's upper shelf,
with the sea a shelf below some traveler's feet.
Planets, time, position line, position line—
and the place is fixed. Invisibly.

If it is to be The Moths, then
something about their flight. April, perhaps.
In a window, the night-blooming horn
of a gramophone. And over the fields,
moths flying, holding their brief shapes
in constant angle to a planet's light.

If it is to be The Waves—the sextant and salt—
then nothing to see at first but stars
and indices. Not the wake's pale seam.
Not a fin or foremast. Not even
the daylit band of the past,
just under the earth's horizon.

. . .

Not yet, at least. No story. (A lamp, perhaps,
a flowerpot.) No past with its child
stopped by a lake in her stiff shoes, toeing
the placid water. Arm's length before her,
in an arc, dollops of bread bob—and beyond
the bread, in a second arc, a dozen,
hand-sized turtles, treading in place.

They cannot eat, the moths. (A little nectar,
a little sap.) Mandibles gone. Just a slender,
tubal tongue wound like a watch spring
in their hollow throats. And, afraid, the turtles
will not eat, the shadow of the backlit child
rippling toward them as, one by one,
new dollops of bread drop.

If it is to be The Waves, then
cycles on cycles. Eternity. Plurality. (Even the rogue

absorbed.) If it is to be The Moths, then
singleness and brevity. Great brevity—although,
in the leaves behind the child, they are just
beginning to stir, the day's late light

caught in the orbs of the early lamps.
And what is that feeling, shaking its wings
within her? Late day, the leaves and bread
and urgency, all the curious curved shapes
treading in place. If she took a step backward,
would they, in an arc, draw nearer, as a ring
might follow its planet? What then
would she make of the world?

Correlation of the Physical Forces

· MICHAEL FARADAY

Watched, as a child, the clockmaker, the glint
of his iris deep in the eyepiece, like mica in a well.

Watched iron filings bristle a magnet.

In his father's shop, watched an axle's tip sag over an anvil.

Loved the Fens.

Loved Virgil's words on young vines, their trellis
of elms in the nursery field.

Considered life as a clockmaker.

Considered life as a blacksmith.

Loved, on his mother's table, the candle-powered carousel,
how the colts floated up on their tiny fobs as the heat rose.

.   .   .

Wrote with pencil in a leather-bound notebook:
"Soap bubbles." "Balloon."

Wrote: "Refer to the last lecture."

Wrote: "Respiration and its analogy
to the burning of a candle."

Considered Virgil's vines, transplanted.

Considered the empty elms, each knife-notched
to show where the vines once faced.

Inducted electrical currents. (Seven halfpence, seven
rounds of zinc, six paper discs moistened by salted water.)

Refuted, through science, séance table-turning.

Saw, through Virgil, notched elms as the map
for a parallel planting.

Understood, as a child, the hiss of a candle's wick.

.   .   .

Understood the clockmaker's words: *verge*, *escapement*.

Loved electromagnetism, "The constant circling of a wire
round a magnet and a magnet round a wire."

Loved the lack of escapement there, each
neither dragging the other nor leaving it behind.

Saw, through Virgil, notched elms as the tracks
of a cogged wheel.

Saw, through time, "The idea of them as they dwell in matter."

Wrote in a blue-green notebook: "Carbon." "Cathode."
"~~Cannot~~." "Cannot." "However exalted they may be."

Wrote: "We shall today." "For a little while."

Wrote: "Correlation of the physical forces."

Exhibition of a Rhinoceros at Venice

· AFTER THE PAINTING BY PIETRO LONGHI, C. 1751

To the tumbler settling on the sawdust street,
with its flames and hoops and carnival swords

swirling up like an alchemist's galaxy, this quiet scene,
glimpsed through a stable's open doors, seems at first

a pond—wall-locked, opaque, lit from above
by the upreaching arc of a white swan.

Then his eyes adjust and the pond is a dampened
stable floor, one ruffle of black rhinoceros. And who

would step forth to restrain him,
if he slipped on his hands and tumbler's knees

in through that black expanse? Or rolled
in a patchwork somersault

. . .

like a moon in its blue orbit, while
the swan slowly shifted from beak and wing

to a gaggle of white-masked spectators, mute in the muted
light? Who would object if he nestled beside

that nobility, that count, that willowy, pale contessa
whose throat and white breast

first gave to his eyes a swan's neck? From her perch
near a waist-high wall, she is watching

a black-cloaked domino, the dip of his tricornered hat
as he bends to the still rhinoceros,

the wall a border he leans across. And who
would not quicken, as the tumbler does

. . .

in his froth of sawdust and shadow, when
the beast slowly raises its earthen mass,

its dusty, furrowed, thick-skinned snout, where
a flag of summer wheat dangles? Just over

its plated hull, just over its rheumy, upturned eyes,
the eyes of the domino hover, dim, plated

in silk, pale as hoops
afloat in some future's flat-lit sky.

Dominance? Challenge? A courtship display?
Who would not wonder what the animal sees

in the white-masked face of such
facelessness, as its toes slowly spread

on the dampened floor, and a shiver of wheat
rises and falls with its breathing?

Accountancy: Dürer in Antwerp

This many times have I dined with the Factor ///////,
thus often with Stecher /, thus with my Lords //////.
(I am drawn to the fishes. And to citrons—sugared,
like frost over gem stones.)

In trade for my portraits, I have taken
a branch of white coral, a cedarwood rosary, an ounce
of good ultramarine. And a great fish scale
that gauzes the day through its intricate lens.

This many times have mummers amused me ////.

Fourteen stuivers, to date, for raisins. Two for a brush.
One for a buffalo horn. Twenty florins in all
for firewood, flax, one elk's hoof, one parrot cage.
In December, four florins—gold—for a little baboon

who nods like Erasmus when darkness descends.
There is solace, I find, in accountancy,

the prudent, resonant thrift of an evening's meal
preserved in a slant mark, like the solace I feel

with needle and ink, Time's cantering beast
furred for eternity by a burin's bite.

To Johann, one *Passion*. To the surgeon
and house servant, each, a *Life of Our Lady*.
To Konrad, in service of the Emperor's daughter,
one *Melancholy*, three *Mary*s, a *Eustace*, a *Nemesis*,
a *Jerome in His Cell*. (Arranged on a wall,
these gifts might mirror our human progression,
as the Great Procession of Our Lady's Assumption—/—
mirrored our ranks, butcher to saint.)

This many times has a fever consumed me /////.
I have dined again // with my Lords.

At the Feast of Our Lady's Assumption, just after
Craftsmen in the Great Procession, but before Prophets
and an armored Saint George, came a crowd of widows
garbed in white linen, accounting for losses amongst us.
Silent, in step, they seemed not shape but vacancy,

.   .   .

alit between mason and seamstress, foot soldier and clerk.

They seemed the space an etch mark frees,

the empty trough that shape awaits.

Grand day, carmine and boot-black and the swirling

world. And those stately widows

defining our borders? These times

did their passing enfold me //////////////////////////////.

Biography

To the dedicated listener, two sounds prevailed that night:
from rafters above the Grand Canal, pigeon snores,
and from the murky water, the tap of gondolas,
like empty walnut shells, against the water steps.
A January Wednesday, 1894, and through those
parenthetic sounds, a figure, Constance Woolson—
novelist, great friend to Henry James—leapt
to her death.

> *She fell.*

Depressed—*delirious, demented*—she died of—*influenza*—
loving him. *Of unrequited love for James? There is no*
evidence. Seven years before that night, mid-April
through late May, they shared a home in Bellosguardo.
A villa. Voluminous. Then met in Geneva, secretly.
Secretly? Perhaps, although discretion ruled, not
impropriety.

> No impropriety? Agreed, although
what ruled was vanity, his need for her devotion.
A spinster, deaf—in just one ear—*and elderly*—a mere

three years his senior—*she was for him primarily a . . .*
source—think Alice, Tita, Cornelia, May—
yes, a loyal friend, of course, but . . .

                    Knowing
her death was suicide, James "utterly collapsed."
He could not know, although he suffered, yes. And moved
into her empty rooms, into her empty beds, in Venice, then
in Oxford. *He sought her ghost—as you do now.*
She took herself away—*There is no evidence—*
away from his possession,

                    he who so valued possession.
What is biography? What did he mourn? *Analysis?*
Appropriation? She slipped away, as he has slipped
from you. *Anecdote and intuition?* Some weeks beyond
her death, by gondola, James ferried her dresses
to the wide lagoon and, one by one—*Reverence?*
Devotion?—

          lowered them into the water.
They floated back, and back, he said—*Hearsay?*

Secondhand remembrance?—like ghastly, black

balloons, empty and full simultaneously;

although, through salt, silt, and the turning years,

their tidal scrape against the weave—

Reciprocal immortality?—there is no evidence.

From Campalto

We entered Venice by Casa degli Spiriti.

• CONSTANCE FENIMORE WOOLSON

Imagine a white horse, alone in a watery meadow.
Or, alone in a watery meadow, imagine
a white horse. The latter increases your need for me,
your relief in my company, as we walk together
down the story's thin lanes, circling the meadow
and lolling horse, and the gondoliers on the landing
bicker and smoke and shuffle their soft-backed cards.
We have, you as my character and I as your guide,
crossed from Venice on the wide lagoon—
rib-cage deep but for trenches the ships slip through—
and we look toward it now, as one by one
its spires sink through a white fog, that, like your need,
advances.

      To keep me beside you, you speak
of da Vinci's menagerie and the grape skins
best suited for grappa. You would question my friendship
with Henry James—you had hoped, in fact,
for Henry James—but I have grown singular here,

essential to you as our gondoliers, although

they've turned silent, fog-erased, and beacon us closer

by nothing but pipesmoke and their cards' arrhythmic

purr. You would ask of his manner, his temperament,

the nature of our fidelity—two writers enamored

with fiction's grip—of my life in his presence,

of my life in his shadow,

                    but are grateful instead

to watch as I pock our trench with pilings

and we feel our way back through the pale lagoon,

column by column, much as the blind

might track the cairns on an ancient path.

You are frightened, I know, in those intervals

when our hands break free and we float

into nothingness. And, yes, I have kept this from you:

increasingly, as the page fills, I am the fabric

of nothingness. You would ask of his voice

and fashion, the nature of our fidelity,

but out from the white fog, here is Casa degli Spiriti,

where up you swing from the swaying boat

and that which remains absorbs me.

Girl in a Dove-Gray Dress

When their slim pirogue slipped over the trapper trails,
through salt marsh and tupelo swamps, out
through inlets and broken bayous, Joseph Mason,
Audubon's border boy, who could paint the backdrops
but not the birds, the surround but not the subject,

cut blossoms from low-hanging branches, filling
the prow. At thirteen (although some said eighteen),
he knew the sea but not the inlets. From rumor
and warped maps, he knew the routes, past branches
and pilings thick with birds—more each day, more

than a single life could paint—he knew the routes
but not the journey, the mission but not the compromise:
The Birds of America abridged by abundance.
Large for his age, or small, what did he know
of compromise? Or of Audubon, slumped

. . .

in the stern, neck stretched down

toward his silent flute, like a great heron

bent forever down an elephant folio? What did he know

of the whole, lessened? How vision, on its path

from the mind to the world, dissipates? For him,

the oak on the shore was the oak on the page.

(But not the waterlogged banyan, its roots

limbs, its shape too reversed for the untrained eye.)

Dead just before forty, he had loved the flat pirogue,

the sleek, mottled, tapered skin that swept him

so weightlessly over the water. And graphite. Chalk.

How paper could hold what held the birds.

He had loved the ibis. And the belladonna—*Its lift*

like a dark cape! (Although what he loved was flight,

not word—and neither within his reach.) As Audubon rallied,

caught what he could, from crane to a speckle

of kinglet, Joseph braided their vine-filled atmospheres,

over then under, in the style of the woven, there

then not, in the style of the frame. Dead long before

forty, his life half absorbed by settings,

.   .   .

he was drawn at last by sitters: the dual exchange
of portraiture. Merchants. Matrons. Then his best,
a child in a dove-gray dress. And although
he rendered her backdrop badly—sewing box
and books stretched out of perspective—

he painted her face with the same precision
he gave to a cut flower, when all he knew of abundance
was filling the prow: an oval of matte, magnolia light,
and, as shadow just starting along one edge,
the slender scorch of compromise the living carry.

Meriwether and the Magpie

Did he know the one as sorrow, the one
he held, gunshot-fallen, its
remarkable long tale . . . beautifully variagated?

For the viewer, fate's in the numbers, legend says:
One magpie for sorrow, two for mirth,
three for a wedding, four for a birth . . .

And wedded in their way they were—Lewis, the bird—
their fragile union finalized *with a narrow ring*
of yellowish black just at the rim of the bird's dim eye.

September. Morning. A breeze
through the aspens, fine. (Five for silver, six for gold . . .)
Two centuries still, until language could cup,

in the binary digits of zero and one, all
it could name. And so he cupped the bird,
and framed in script its glossy frame:

. . .

the belly is of a beatifull white . . . the wings . . .
party coloured . . . changeable . . . sonetimes presenting as . . .
orange yellow to different exposures of ligt.

Time still, until sorrow's variegated wing
would bisect the land, would sever from the whole
each singular figure. Here was wonder,

chipped from the western sky, its legs and taloned toes,
black and imbricated, the shifting tint of its shape,
particolored, changeable. (Seven for a secret not to be told.)

The wings have nineteen feathers . . . it's usual food
is flesh . . . beautifull . . . yellow . . . a redish indigo blue . . .
at this season single as the halks.

September, the little rhyme fluttering above him,
dragging in from the far Atlantic its swift, domestic echo.
Did he wonder, then, why the story closed so suddenly?

.   .   .

(Eight for heaven, nine for hell, and ten

for the devil's own self.) Why abundance alone

could stop the heart's progression?

Morning. Nine's beak, eight's weightless wings.

Then ten, heartless with promise, sets down

on a dipping branch, the click of its digits—

black and imbricated—beginning

the cycle again: the one and then the nothing

from which the one sets forth.

Incomplete Lioness

Or lion. Too little marble left for certainty:
affixed to a bonelike armature, just a flank
and scored shoulder, and far down the missing,
crouching shape, a single, splay-toed paw.
The companion, or mate, is better formed
and offers a template to trace a bit, image to absence
to memory, until the lioness fills.

The exhibit is *Fragments and Dislocations:*
Sight and Sightlessness. Across the room
in Renaissance, the painter, retinas tattered
as a saint's hem, might have filled the lioness
differently: absence first, then memory,
and then the lines around his own vision, its crags

and wilderness. His century failed him,
a placard says. Just eyelid balms
and powdered rhubarb. What retina remained
must have caught the subject's chosen states—penitence

and ecstasy—nearsightedly, which would explain
the perfect stones, less perfect trees. Or perhaps
his partial sightlessness was corneal, and thus

the painting's mood, front-lit through gauze.
In either case, what the painter knew—that his saint
and tiny crucifix would not adorn an altarpiece—
comes to us more slowly. Wood grains,
punch patterns, and the small keyhole
beneath a varnished leaf, suggest a sacristy cupboard,

not worship's place, but preservation's.
Chosen states, the placard said.
Vacancy and memory. Ecstasy and penitence.
And then, *His partial vision of the whole*
produced a partial masterpiece:
a saint—Jerome—and grizzled robe, flawless
in its dust. The rest is incomplete, but zero-mass

radiography, its lights and darks reversed,
reveals a shape beneath the scene:
Jerome as just two simple lines, white arc

across white axis—before they both were white-

washed over, and the saint began,

and umber brought the lion to him.

On Reflection

• MICHAEL FARADAY

I will never contain the whole of it, he said,
the mirror too small for the long-necked lamp
floating swanlike near the angle of incidence.
Never, he said, stepping back from the lectern

and long-necked lamp, the mirror he held too small
for the swan. To reflect the object entirely,
he said, stepping back to the lectern,
the glass must be half the source's height.

To reflect the object entirely—the lamp,
or a swan, or my figure before you—
the glass must be half the source's height.
Unlike thought, which easily triples the whole.

My figure before you, the lamp's swan,
reflects my object entirely; that is, unlike
thought, which easily triples—or transforms—the whole,
the mirror is bound by harmony.

. . .

Entirely. Unlike the object reflected.
Finally, when you back away from the glass, your image—
the mirror is bound by harmony—
always doubles the distance between you.

As it finally backs away through the glass,
light doubling its loss through angles of reflection,
your image doubles the distance between you—always
twice as far from the source as you are before it:

Like a thought doubly lost through an act of reflection
floating swanlike past its angle of incidence,
twice as far from its mate as a lamp from a mirror
that will never contain the whole of it.

PART THREE

Roget's Illusion: Three

In Roget's first edition, slimmer by half
than this last, the whole is closer to folly,
the part to wisdom, the start to the close,

although, short or long, the journey's the same—
begin with *Existence* and end in the cloisters—
and, early or late, *Space, Matter,*
Sensation, Volition, like navigable stars,
direct us, expansion by expansion.

Sunlight this morning. April. And twice,
when a sudden breeze crossed over my desk,
the 19th century's yellowed pages lifted like wings,
the later version flapping behind, a tissue-thin flurry
of words spinning into their antonyms.

Then everything settled
back into neighboring columns: *birth*
and *cessation, advent* and *flight, source*

．　．　．

and *consequence*. In a work of this nature,

Roget wrote—the cocoon of language forever

swelling—*Perfection* exists as far

from *Attainment* as *deity* from *galaxy*.

But not far at all from *Imperfection*.

Or *Blemish*. Or *Bane*. List beside list,

like rain-filled furrows they shape each other—

and together hatch, just between *blight*

and *flawlessness*, a rust-tipped moth

that sips from each continually.

Steller's Jay

• GEORG STELLER, THE AMERICAN EXPEDITION, 1742

From the Harbor of Apostles Peter and Paul,

we sailed in their namesakes, *St. Peter*

with its groats and falconets, *St. Paul*

with its groats and falconets,

then ship and ship in a topgallant wind

bearing east-southeast together, identical to the distant eye

as glimmer and reflection.

. . . .

When we shall wish to speak to you, Captain—and Captain—

to warn you or guide you or follow or precede you,

we shall, through pennants, jacks, drums, bells,

lanterns, guns, and speaking horns,

deliver a language precise as script,

through which may God preserve us.

. . . .

Light rain. Open sea.

.   .   .

I think of the rhumb we have set for ourselves
as ice upon a pin tip: point and course
interchangeable.
                        Now and then,
from the pitch pot, the faintest scent of pine.

St. Paul in the east all morning.

. . . .

If we should desire that you take the lead . . .
If you should desire to lower the yards . . .
If it is desired to anchor in fog . . .
If we should separate—
from which misfortune may God preserve us . . .
If after three days . . .
If from the flagstaff a blue flag . . .
If in sailing close-hauled or free . . .

. . . .

What good is structure against a world
already structured by chaos? What good,
pattern, sequence, formation, formality?
We lost the *St. Paul* on the sixteenth day,
though we sensed thereafter a parallel presence.

. . .

Four months. Clewed, hove to.

Then islands and islands at the New World's rim.

What else can I tell you?

Shipwreck. Rocks on the boot soles. Down the beach,

one arctic fox, fearless, barked.

. . . .

Presence? Parallel. A thereafter sensed. We, though . . .

. . . .

Then more, barking, white in their winter fur,

slinking in toward our fires like ground fog.

They had no history with us, and hence

no fear of us, we with so little but history.

We shot them. They came. We shot. They came.

When winter blew through our crude huts,

we caulked the sticks with their bodies.

When blizzards drove us deep in their caves,

they climbed into crevices over our heads, shifting

all night like a wind-rippled canopy—

or wide-winged, otherworldly bird
that would not fly from us.

. . . .

When we shall lay to . . . you shall lay to . . .
When we after drifting . . . you after drifting . . .
When we shall lower . . . you shall lower . . .

. . . .

To lay, drifting lower. After drifting
to rise . . . As, God willing, they do, sounding their way
down these shallow coasts, echo by echo.

Scurvy and winter lessened us, already
halved on the sixteenth day—
not from ourselves, exactly, or from others,
but from the outcome of self and other,
the crafted, patterned offerings
that, over water, met us halfway.

What else can I tell you, there in your morning
or nightfall, knowing already
of voyages, violence, hardship, grace? What else

can I write, alive and whole and world-full,

yet fractured as these notes to you?

From the body of our ship, collapsed on the shore,

we built a ship, from the shattered shape

a smaller shape, a single-masted oval cask

which, over time, delivered us.

. . . .

Two lanterns, that we might receive you . . .

Six guns, that we might avoid you . . .

One flag—blue—that we might know you

after long absence . . .

. . . .

They seem nothing but steam now, the foxes.

The sudden, unbidden breath over glass

that blinds us shapelessly.

What most endures with me—

a multivoiced jay—will, you say,

carry what most remains of me. My name

and the bird stitched back to back, balanced

．　．　．

as reflection. *S-t-e-l-l-e-r-'-s j-a-y*—

four strokes plus a star mark reaching upward,

five strokes in answer close to the ground,

one stroke, then one

fathoming, and the whole,

                    aloft on the thermals,

blue as the pennants that reveal from the crosstrees

we are each the lost companion.

Details Depicted:
Insect and Hair

In the prison of an unnamed century,

on paper coarse as sackcloth,

someone has written *No reason exists*

and *the innocency of my actings*

in midst of the late revolutions.

Then stopped—and circled two perfect artifacts,

caught years before in the damp pulp:

in the margin beside his curving *s*,

a single fly wing, dried to a gauze,

and far down the page, an arc of amber beard hair.

And as he writes for leniency, for his place

within the fabric of place, *the stars*

above this terraqueous globe and *the hazel wheat*,

he wishes the wing had followed the hair,

as transcendence follows the life well lived.

He wishes the order reversed—

that, first, lit by the hair's prophetic glint,

he might open his story—*Born of worthy parents*—

then weave his history forward, as the paper itself

wove history forward: flax to fabric to shirt
(pockets emptied, buttons snipped) to boiler to pulp
to lifted chin. He knows the power
of augury, of the signs in a *perfect path*.
He knows, were the wing pinned
near the page's end, he might close
with the grand intangibles, the diaphanous *strivings*
of citizenship—freedom, peace,
benevolence—and earn,
by his words, his flight.

                              Late day,
on the wind, two bells ringing in tandem,
sound and echo indistinguishable. No help
at all, the artifacts. Or augury. What good
is transcendence *before* the body, the natural,
upward arc reversed? As useless now
to elevate his humanness as to watch
the cobbled page withdraw, regain its rags,
its sacking, rope, its bits of salted fishing net.
If only time had stalled the fly—
and wing and hair were closer—his words
might ride them seamlessly, as sound

rides the ringing bells—*globe* and *glint* and *citizenship*
indistinguishable on the wind.

If only weight

were valued more than weightlessness.
But pulp has fastened each to its place
and he has encircled them.

Enthusiasm

B. mori: an inconspicuous moth, stout, weak-winged . . .
larvae hairless, hook-tailed . . . second thoracic ring
humped . . . and from the spinnerets, three thousand feet
of silk thread. Here Pasteur quickened, the book's words
stepping down to his favorite word, enthusiasm—
the god within—which, in its bald, Bombyxian way,
even the moth might feel as *Rhythmically turning*
in figure eights three hundred thousand times,
the ash-gray larval head casts its looped cocoon.

It was a time of cheap bread and parties,
grand public works and conspiracies. He quickened,
looked out at the palace trees, enthusiasm for the words—
and works—rising within him: the tireless heads
that spat the silk or cinched the empiry. He felt it,
there on the palace balcony, the god within,
the god who loped through the huntsmen's hounds
or gasped in the Empress's throat
as she bent to his microscope's eyepiece

and saw within not the god but the world,
its spores and languid flagellates.

Benign, but related to the injurious lackeys.
Mulberry-feeding . . . reproduction continuous
in the warmer reaches. Pasteur nodded. It was a time
of injurious lackeys. Across the land, cocoons collapsed
and shriveled larvae peppered the lip-cast industry.
He nodded, enthusiasm for the moths, the cause, the cure,
tapped like a pulse beneath his pulse, rose in that dusk
as it always rose, season to season, past germs and bacilli
and parasites, even as he understood that the anti-life
infection shaped, the unmaking
that it patterned, was every inch as intricate
as the silk that drooped from an Empress's throat.

Now the moon appeared, pale in the palace trees.
He closed his book. In the courtyard below his balcony,
torch-bearing huntsmen were forming a large ring, one hunter

at the center, like a moon in a circle of stars. And again

it rose, enthusiasm for the ring, the hunter

now lifting skyward the dark, ceremonial flank of a stag.

Pasteur felt it again tapping as into the ring

the hunt hounds crept, then stopped, crept, stopped, crept,

stopped: enthusiasm for the ring, the hounds, the man within

who three times stopped them with a word.

Enthusiasm for the word, even when his counterword—

so close in sound, just an octave higher—

released them to the meat.

Darwin's Mirror

He placed a small mirror between his study windows. . . .

Through reflection, he could watch me approaching,

down the curved lane from gate to door, as I,

looking back, imagine him rising from his wide chair,

and a bit of the hearth and foot cushion.

Whenever weather mottled the mirror, Comfort—

then Lettington—polished it, clipping back the foliage

to a living frame that held us equally. And then

I was in, walking behind him down the wide hall

and across the back veranda, then out

toward his sandwalk copse. The mirror bent down

from the outer wall much as the mirror at Saint Bartholomew's

bends down from the organist's loft. And I told him this,

as we moved past the phlox and portulacas

and the ghostly rattle of the well's flywheel circled

behind us like locusts. From my pew in the empty church,

. . .

I knew that the mirror carried signals
up from choirmaster to loft—and didn't reflect
the organist's fingers down to the congregation, although

I imagined both, their seamless display cast down to me
through a slender cone of dust. Descent with modification—
but that is his phrase, not mine. And this

is his making: a long and narrow oval
shading a meadow's outer rim: a copse of hazel,
dogwood, hornbeam, birch, their leaves, as we walk

through the seasons, first a rasp then a rattle.
History is closer now, I say. And did he know that crows,
perched in the northern regions, gather

a little arc of ice on—what is it called? Just under
the throat? Gorget, he says. Yes, on the puffed gorget.
The ice looks like a queen's ruff. Or half-ruff,

nothing at the back, of course. In the hazel
just over our heads, the bird waits for a moment, regal
in its ruff of ice: a dark shape

. . .

we fashion together, gorget, black eye in a membrane
of lid. And although we know the ruff ends
where breath stops, we finish the circle anyway.

The Moths

• VIRGINIA WOOLF, 1940

Up through the war they stream, the blunt bombers,
rushing toward her unbidden between tea and dinner—
but no, the *moths* rushed toward her unbidden,
and years before, lovely, alit by the same luminous windows

she papered just this morning. After her walk on the marsh.
When guns rumbled on the Channel ports. But no,
it was thunder that rumbled, although under the storm
the guns of Flanders softly popped.

How the war obsesses. And she cannot form letters,
or forms them as echoes, words drawn back
through the years, their figures confused. No, fused—
for hadn't the Messerschmitt, crashed on Caburn's summit,

crowned the mountain like a blunt moth, wings extended?
There's petrol saved for suicide, Leonard said,
should Hitler win. And on the lilacs? Perfect
summer weather. So they go on. Panic, then bowls

on the green lawn. The buzz of propellers just overhead
and, at sunset, the glow of Botten's haystack.
Midway through her walk, when the air-raid siren bleated,
she looked to the haystack for refuge—a filigree

of camouflage—but no, the sky stayed clear
and she hurried on. Once, Duncan said, near Charleston,
high in the cloudless sky, he watched a bomber crumble—
instantly—just a flash and almost silent click.

Sunset. A wash of poppies in the corn. And do moths
circle the haystack's almost light, as bombers circle
the almost seen? One weighted, one weightless,
one poisoned, one benign, bracketing the hour?

She cannot form letters. Looks out
through the marsh. Had she entered the sweet hay,
rewoven its skein above her, dropped back
and back through the years, until she was nothing

.   .   .

but cells in a larval slick, would the soul reopen,

borderless? But no—always—the outer bracket

closes. High in the cloudless sky, Duncan said,

silver pencil, puff of smoke.

Salvage

What was the sound, a rasp?
No, not a rasp. *A rattle, then?* No, not that.
And twice it passed over you? I sat
at the waist-gunner window. Night—
and the wingtip's flashing light
bit through slanted snow: green, green.
Then we struck the mountain. *And of eight,*
five were thrown free and survived?
I was cast into deep snow
and plane-shaped debris slipped over me.
Its sound a scraping? No,
not a scraping. It slipped down the canyon wall
and I followed its snow-trough, then
guided the others to me
with blasts from my Mae West whistle.
Yours was a rescue mission, far from war?
I was alone and just overhead in the darkness
snow geese and trumpeter swans passed.
And the green light flashed?

I could hear their bodies working—*And you sat*
at the waist?—ligament, ligature, the labor
of leaving. *In unison, then? A thrum?* No,
each sound in its slender chamber. *And you*
whistled them down to you? Yes.

The Swifts

One August night, ten thousand.
Four thousand now, in this long, September dusk.
Some repeaters, staying over.

No first-growth stumps in sight—
no forests at all on this stretch of flyway—
and so they roost in a school's brick chimney,
ten thousand then, four thousand now,

turning in wide, counterclockwise gyres
above the chimney's rusted clockface, turning
their four-inch, half-ounce shapes, three heartbeats
per wingbeat, three heartbeats per clipped syllable
of each high-pitched cry, some repeaters,

staying over. Just to the west,
the sunset that stains their bellies
to the dusty gold of mine canaries

. . .

slips over the gray Pacific, which to the east, under
Kentucky and Illinois, the root-tips of fossil forests
reach down through the roofs of coal-mine shafts.
Tropical then, the trees, three hundred million years ago,

rain-filled, before the planet quickly warmed
and the magma shifted and the world's first birds
cast their first neuronic blips
and the world's first flocks answered in unison.
What? the miners asked, brushed on the nape

by a weightlessness three hundred million years
whittled. Only the roots of absence, tepid
across the skin. And tangible in that darkness

as the sudden blip that any moment now
will draw this flock, like airborne ash, backward
through the chimney. The cell-phone camera eyes,
like miners' headlamps, tip up in unison

toward a micro-ounce of source too swift
for mystery. Wing dip? Cell click? Could the answer
be corporeal? Attention to the matter?

Their eyes are bigger than their beaks. Their sleep—
no opposable toes—is vertical. Just to the west,

a line of contrail draws us—
and down they drop, wings tucked, past
the chipped mortar and carbon dust, past the open flue,
the first birds overlapped by the next, and those

by the next, and next, climbing the chimney's shadow shape
in four-inch repetitions. Ten thousand then,
four thousand now, upright on the bricks.

Pierrots, Slightly Leaning:
Brighton, 1915, Venice, 1903

· AFTER PAINTINGS BY WALTER SICKERT

War. Desire. In painting one, the last hours
brighten the wind-blown gas lamps, which light in turn
a wooden stage and beach chairs, a slouched pierrot
alert to an absent audience. In painting two

no Brighton at all, no gas lamps' down-turned light
wind-blown to gull wings. Just costumed lovers—two—
alert to an absent audience. In painting two, embracing,
the shadowed figures fuse, he in white—his wizard's cap

and gull-wing sleeves—loving the role, accustomed to
the secrecy, she in black, back toward us, a darkened
figure fused to white, shadowed by a wizard's cap.
The time in painting one is war. Behind the knock-down stage

the sea creeps toward us, sheened in black, a darkened
hush climbing a darkened pier. Across the Channel, the guns

of Flanders—the time in painting one is war, the stage
is European, a knock-down shape shattered and regathered—

across the Channel, the guns of Flanders softly pop.
The time in painting two is here—and here—a classic, transient
shape, a knock-down *now* forever shattered and regathered.
The white pierrot leans slightly forward, his lover—here

and here a classic, transient shape—leans slightly back.
It's Venice, evening, moonlight pale on a black canal.
The Brighton pierrot leans forward slightly, dragging
his oiled form across a brushstroke of air.

It's England, evening, moonlight pale on the black channel. . . .
And beyond the frames but within the moment, something stutters
homeward, dragging an oily line across the prop-stroked air
or swimming in circles down a shoreless canal.

. . .

Beyond the frames but within the moment, something stutters
homeward—toward some perfect, restive memory, some lost hush
drifting in circles through a shoreless *now*.
Within the prop- and paw-fed strokes, beyond

the hush, the silent, restive harmony,
past the wooden stage and beach chairs, the slouched pierrots,
out from the prop- and paw-fed lappings, still
it struggles on. The last of our wars is desire.

The Shepherd's Horn

I am imagining how it would be if we could infuse souls.

• VIRGINIA WOOLF

I.

Then moonlight burned through the low fog
and back he came, the gondolier, first
head and torso bent over the long oar, then
black shoes, soft on the stern's worn track.
And Wagner, his back to the prow, saw it all
as a slow unveiling, the figure moving
his huge sweep and, behind him, the spires
and funnel-shaped chimneys, then the marbled walls
and porticoes, then at last, all along the canal,
the black-cast, algae-slick stairs, stepping
down through the lapping water. And then,
Wagner wrote, sound drew what moonlight had drawn:
From the gondolier a wail began, not unlike the cry
of an animal, and slowly strengthened and formed itself
from long-drawn "Oh!" to the simple notes "Venezia."
And the sound, Wagner wrote, revealed the place,

and the place the past, and the past the echo

that, like the watery sweep of an oar, carried him

backward into the future and became, in turn,

the long-drawn wail of the shepherd's horn

at the launch of *Tristan*'s third act.

II.

A meadow, with sheep.

Lifting the gramophone's ebony arm,

Leonard said how the horn, the shepherd's horn,

once again brought back his childhood.

And the painting, high on the dining room wall,

a meadow, with sheep. And although Wagner's opera

rejects the daylit world, its false revelations, still,

Leonard said, the horn recalls that daylit scene,

widening as the note holds—how, here and there,

paint buckled like sealing wax and textured

the sheep. Then the real sunlight, how it brought

from the wooden floor a dozen amber currents,

and, from the carpet where he sat, a woolen garden.

III.

Blank. The land today was a canvas,

blank. No shepherd, no sheep. Just frost.

Burning white, Virginia said. *Burning blue.*

Then the elms, red. And what was that phrase

she forgot to remember? *Look your last*

on all things lovely. The war brings a sharp,

immediate sorrow. *Tavistock Square is no more.*

It swells, then fades, as urgent sorrow must.

Then through a shallow wash of sunlight,

high on a slender elm, some deeper, cosmic sadness

opens its blunt wings. Then it too . . . somehow . . . lifts.

Red, purple, dove blue grey. I did not mean

to describe, once more, she said, *the downs in snow.*

But it came.

IV.

His childhood garden seemed touched by snow,

although it was August, each long-abandoned brittle stalk

chafed to dust. No sound as he stood there, Leonard said,

no wind. He was five. *The grimy ivy drooped*

on the grimy walls. And across the walls,

from leaf to leaf, were dozens and dozens

of spiderwebs, each pocked by a bead of spider.

And it came to him then for the first time,

that cosmic sorrow she mentioned—when

all of the windows are dark down the street,

and the dust is unmoving,

and desire fails.

V.

To transcend desire, Tristan said, transcend

the world. Then Wagner placed him in a castle garden,

under a lime tree, downstage from a castle gate,

and said to him, *Now you are home,*

amidst your meadows and delights, in the light

of the old sun. And Tristan answered,

Is there any anguish

which it does not revive in its beams?

VI.

Then it too . . . somehow . . . lifts.

VII.

Why try again to make the familiar catalogue?
The frost, the elms, the colors, red, blue, dove grey?
She had written, Virginia said, *Last night*
a great heavy plunge of bomb under the window—
and then, directly thereafter, of the elm tree's leaves
against the sky, of the cows feeding, of the pear tree
swagged with pears. Beauty. Pity. *Why try again*
to make the familiar catalogue,
from which something always escapes?

VIII.

From which something always escapes.
And shall they listen again to the opera's first notes,
their rise and fall, like long oars inching a ship
toward Cornwall? And did he remember their walk
years ago?—the line of straw they placed near the river
to measure its height. Fog, thick on the water.

A boatman's voice, far down the towpath.

Why try again? Morning. Rooks in the trees.

How she had written, *The deer exactly match*

the bracken. And then they do not. How over the water

a horn sounded, then a deer escaped its camouflage

and fled up the steep embankment.

For better or worse, beauty or pity—did he remember?—

how that bounding shape broke free.